DARK
STAR
SUNFLOWER

Poems by
DARRELL EPP

First Edition

Cover art: Wassily Kandinsky, *Merry Structure*
Cover design by Matthew J. Distefano
Interior layout by Matthew J. Distefano

Print ISBN 978-1-964252-55-1
Electronic ISBN 978-1-964252-56-8

Printed in the United States of America

 QUOIR

Published by Quoir
Chico, California
www.quoir.com

Imagination of some great exploit drives
him beyond the bound of patience.

— William Shakespeare

Contents

Also by Darrell Epp

Alien Phonics Primer
Permanent Smoke
Mechanical Monkeys
Sinners Dance
After Hours
Imaginary Maps

How to Build a River

don't open that email: i know it's spam by
its meat-byproduct slaughterhouse smell.
don't try dreaming until you've logged
10,000 hours in the flight simulator:
too risky. some men never return.
i've seen it happen. the grenade was
just a toy but the explosion was real.
and how could mom just march us off
to war like that? a cookie, a hug, a
new enemy just over the hill. wish
i could still believe in magic lamps
and happy endings. bizarro talking
backwards makes more and more
sense as gravity grinds our towers
back into powder. they replaced the
river with a formula for a river, now
i can't even give a flying kick to a
glass door without feathers flying
everywhere. recipe for a rock,
styrofoam rock, symbolic rock—
all i wanted was a real rock i
could sink my teeth into. echo
of a radio carved out of crystal:
any memory is a kind of battery.

Honorary Vampire

a problem makes you forget a problem,
and the electric sunset's my best friend.
not fully vampire but mirrors make me
gag for an army of very good reasons.
can't believe heather shot down a giraffe
just for the instagram likes, can't believe
i can't believe it. at least i never joined a
cult, and jury duty and pension plans are
still, to me, vague legendary dreamlands.
if the first man started paying a dollar a
day a million years ago, he still couldn't
pay off the loans of the last man, that's
why i don't call economics a science. i
apologize to the neanderthals; only the
the wind, my second skin, shouts back.
a wrong number shouldn't hurt so much.
gord tries to trick his nemesis by taping
his old factory i.d. badge onto a blowup
doll and leaving it out on the porch—
decoy of a dark fate. my mouth says
good luck, my secret self says i don't
think it works that way. careful with that
gun, it might not be loaded. be careful
with that magnet, my blood is full of iron.

Amazing Twist-Off Head!

some days you wake up feeling like
there's an elephant on your head.
then it turns out the elephant *is* your
head, and you can't remember if the
world is out there or in here, end up
changing your name to galaxy-brain.
drunk santa shot down over area 51,
seasons in hell on hi-def blu-ray dvd,
now with special features. deadbeat
angels rolling dice in limbo's lobby;
the minutes i wasted crying over a
prayer request from a chatbot. she
knew all my magic words. fake
sincerity is such a superpower
when you live in the valley of the
shadow of the pig iron foundry. i
blew my stelco shot with too many
sick days and too many questions.
that was then. now it's padlocks
for miles, paper doll chains of
smirking case workers, labyrinths
carved out of slag-flavored smoke.
expired promises of nefarious oxides:
even our phantoms reek of benzene.

Cro-Mag Serenade

every morning, eye of a sky like a dead
balloon. between sherman and sanford
the centuries catch up with me, roll out
a fresh quicksand pit that's just my size.
my face hurts: it's ifrah again, disguised
as frost. one night we were so sure we
had found the haunted thin places that
divide the river from the bay, the bay
from lake ontario. we tried anything
once but melted cheese on my oreos
was a bridge too far. i got high marks
in ringing random doorbells, looking
for a mentor, a mint condition father
figure action figure. that nexus—
haunted by goblins—where the
underground river changes direction:
i must have left the recipe around
here somewhere. life's a hospital
when we wanted a carnival, with
giggling muppets on the palliative
care sony bravia google tv. bottle
full of burst bubbles, fates as final
as stone age bible verses painted
on space age nuclear warheads.

Endorphin Ballet

covertly, small talk with a stranger prepares
me for a lonely date with destiny: centuries
from now, will transhuman historians refer
to my rock bottom as their golden age? i
dream of passing unnoticed, like melting
icicles or faded billboards, through the
dreary plot twists of my own life. imagine
passing the online screening process
and starting over as that ray of light
banging on hoods of rented cars,
laughing and then moving on. you
saw it too: a fiery muse beyond all
vocabularies. all matter is just frozen
light: i tell myself this when my head
hits the bottom of the canyon and it
barely hurts at all. just another trick i
learned from the old magician, along
with holding my breath until life starts
making sense and nodding my head
to lunchroom sports scores when who
cares, my team isn't playing, my team
is invisible and two universes over. in
memory's jenga-web jungle sleeps
a key that would have unlocked it all.

Poison Lake Honeymoon Suite

ancient birds, tainted by strontium and
uranium from distant nuclear blasts,
lean into the storm, they don't fight it. *our
best days are behind us,* the candidate
says, reddens, remembers the hotel by
the poison lake where his lost the ring.
the voters hunger for easy answers, an
officer chooses the wrong chokehold.
it all feels like a movie, like watching
his own reptile brain transform into
a monstrous imposter, a wicked twin. i
can get used to anything except normal.
it's all the beauty that trips me up, and
what if the thin spots on butterfly wings
are holy windows? you squint hard and
every teardrop's an underwater empire;
a chimney is some angel's emergency
exit. *that's not what i meant,* he says,
*but so what? the way she would hold
her breath as she made a ponytail at
the top of her head, kabuki-style, that's
what i really want to talk to you about.
this economy's all imaginary anyhow,
like a river in a dream,* then falls silent.

Smile-Shaped Puddle

i think i read too many books. too late
now! says the heroine's long-lost twin,
just before the thriller's climax. no going
back. no lifeboat without the death of a
tree, of a seed, of a pregnant supernova.
the villain explains his plan to the beat
of the doomsday clock's tick-tock.
something about magnetism, and
nanobots poisoning the reservoir. i'm
sorry, i thought this was act three!
turns out we're barely halfway there,
and robotech boulevard's just a really
bad painting. get what you pay for,
rip the bandaid off the year's best
scab, baffle the subprime lender
with spicy knock-knock jokes. i
never looked before i leaped.
check the index: diving boards
and mushroom clouds loom large
in my autobiography. my idea of a
brick weighs more than a brick;
wing of a song, nothing at all.
next time let's rehearse first, with
lego blocks and crash helmets.

Suburban Cortex of Regret

the highlight reel's out of focus, crucial
hocus pocus is encrypted, restricted to
paid subscribers only. next time get a
second opinion before signing in blood.
oven-fresh memes invade the darkling
brain, conquer battalions of synaptic
gaps without firing a shot. nicorette-
flavored blizzard, social cues tricky as
math—every hello feels like drawing
a hotel with infinite rooms without the
benefit of tracing paper. and talk about
suspense—a kitkat wrapper sailing
from the puddle to the gutter lurched,
ran aground, sank below the water
line in excruciating slo-mo. i thought
about extinction events, moby dick
and the long goodbye. there were
asbestos flakes in the cereal bowl,
murder on tv. choke on the plastics
in grandma's old-tyme recipe, wake
up screaming from the dream of
overdue homework. must be a map
around here somewhere. all my
favorite continents are imaginary.

Trans-Warp Daffodil Heart

how happy i was, happy as a rock,
before the forceps pinched my skull,
replaced my angel language with
wait times are longer than usual, the
fiendish jargon of debits and credits.
treading water in the dark, dead
man's float in the endless amnion
and the doctor never even warned
me. *sure knows how to cry,* he said,
and the world was upside down.
imagine a party being over before
i even knew the word for 'over.'
like that summer: amber bobby pin
on the dashboard, ice cream stains
on corduroy jeans. goodbye letter
spackled with glitter. i bet on fewer
blind leaps, don't argue religion with
telephone poles anymore either. an
old-timer hums the same ancient
melody, there are secrets too big
for any syllable to hold, and isn't it
wild how birds build their houses
with their mouths? stare at a flower
long enough, it turns into a world.

Love Theme with Bleeding Gums

spent a semester trying to staple soap
bubbles to the wall, only to find i just
don't have the knack. blooming
smokestacks, hit and miss harvest
of iron sulfide. that spiky-headed
thistle, i swear it was a mirror, and
your seat belt warranty's void when
the high-speed collision's' between
your ears. can't really relate to
people who've never crazy-glued
themselves to the eye in the sky,
the carnivorous man in the moon.
what i'm saying is words have wings,
and wings have consequences. frost
grows between my toes. monday's
clown wears a skinsuit made of light.
the brutal sine wave of dating apps,
limbo's bitter bounty, the terms of
service nobody bothered to read.
she said every seed is a miracle,
initiated me into ancient mysteries.
turns out every bit of our data has
a name, and every name hides a
secret jewel that will live forever.

In the Event of Rapid Descent

the horse dreams of unicorns, the worm
wants to be a dragon and, baffled by
upgrades to the self-checkout lane, the
real me is a secret song a mile away.
retail associates are standing by
but their hourly rate is so low their
smiles must be cardboard cutouts.
no wonder our thoughts never quite
touch, ellipsis in the climax, stealth
bomber with a payload of confetti.
hawks flood the radar screen and
the new recruit thinks they're ufo's.
turns out that world-shaped shadow
on my lung x-ray isn't just regret,
that's why stairs are a killer and
tiny elves dance in the pocket
between my eye and the world.
the day has a face like the night
has a face. a rocket blasts off,
wonderboy catches it on his way
to mars. it's dark up there but
wherever we fly we bring more
darkness with us. legend of life,
how i love your bitter aftertaste.

Galaxy Carved out of Plastic

there's another book—not this one—
where you shout the sacred syllable
that allows you to rip the sky in half, to
hear the thoughts of your favorite rock.
magic words; common as table salt.
leading man plot twists flooding the
gutters. but no one believes in that
book anymore. there are scarecrows
hogging all the window seats, the
carnival barker's missing a face and
i'm the reason pencils have erasers.
in every atom there's a secret agent.
i love how the lakebed fits the lake,
how the sky swaddles the 5g tower.
dreams of conquest melt in the heat,
dreams of the womb melt in the heat.
universe with a leaky transmission,
sos at the bottom of the cereal bowl.
breakfast is a glass of i-told-you-so
juice, lunch is a dog with my heart
in its mouth, swimming across the
river of forgetfulness. tinfoil scar.
bumper crop of wrong numbers.
even the pillowcases draw blood.

Origami Staircase

and when the leaves change colors i start to
cry, put my faith in any random theory.
maybe my soul will heal itself, maybe the
devil gives refunds. sami's a flat-earther
now, doesn't think the moon is real. i'm
not sure anything is real, but i sure wish
i still had my old toys, they were magical.
the city sucks its thumb, sheds its skin.
missing stencils from ancient storefronts:
broken symbols from a bygone alphabet.
irving hats—vacant for half a century now;
the future—idling furiously at the red light.
soon becomes too soon as lunar morphs
into lunatic. the story wrote the writer,
never had the heart to set him straight.
steering wheels he twisted so manfully,
just zero-shaped fields of air molecules.
tonight it's dorothee's pulse versus our
doomsday clock's tik-tok, half-life of
the atom's heart versus the ticking
time-bomb. falling upwards into the
true kingdom, sacred rivers full of sky,
pain of a wish turned inside out,
secret city in the white of her eye.

Screaming Trees

sometimes i'm symbolic but not today.
i exist. mom, dad, ghost of a hollow
moon. school as a barrier to learning.
jobs, and the lonely gaps between.
then they invented ear buds—trees
could be screaming and we'd never
even know. outer space is so quiet,
it bothers me, can't believe we sold
those astronauts a one-way ticket.
dear earth: i take it all back, you're
my favorite planet after all. dear
mastercard: catch me if you can.
i learned a new word today:
renoviction. let the landlord count
his coins: we'll build a treehouse,
feather our nest with junk mail
and remaindered bestsellers.
once there was a fire escape
under a crazy quilt of stars, i
had a stutter, your lips were
cinnamon. lilacs wilting in the
static, victory march of the
mayor's bulldozer. love still
wins is all i was trying to say.

Faulty Data from Head Office

details erode until our faces resemble
heads of caesars on ancient coins.
middle of the road, meet middle finger.
i deserved most, but not all, of dad's
spankings. it's too late to ask 1981
for a rematch. the torture garden we
built out of toothpick-sized crutches,
i'll just have to learn to carry it. can't
believe we ever thought math could
explain everything. neanderthal
darrell never never got lost in an
empty room or second-guessed
the sunrise. i miss that guy! he
always knew just what not to say.
to know thyself and not run away,
no matter how many pianos are
throw off how many balconies. to
stare right into the eye of the no
trespassing sign until it turns into
a mirror. yesterday i couldn't stop
laughing, tonight dorothee works
late. all her atoms are mysteries to
me, with names i don't know, but
what i don't know could fill a world.

Redemption Mirage

my icepick turns into an icicle at the worst
possible times. when i pray the sky holds
its breath, waiting for the punchline, but
i forgot to supersize the combo, this
particular club-footed post-jobs tragedy
doesn't come with a laugh track. back
in the day i was always giving strangers
wrong directions: hope they got home ok.
whenever cops would dig a corpse out of
a glacier i'd always check to see if it
looked familiar. i wish i could explain.
i wish tomorrow came with a crash pad.
throw a pot of boiling water into a blizzard
and the scream of steam scalds the air,
the sizzle's like a reformed sinner's
testimony but maybe redemption's just a
really good story, like how the world, with
vast gears you can set your watch by, is
a story. i like the story about the villain
who changes his ways after coming
face to face with a blooming hibiscus;
all that beauty is too much to bear.
he makes amends, he makes a friend,
falls in love with the man in the moon.

Easy as Finding Your Keys in a Snowstorm

ran into an old co-worker, shoeless now
and ranting about the globalists. another
one tried to sell me a timeshare. i told
him, if i *had* any time, i wouldn't share it.
even the valedictorian, peel back the
tinfoil and he's just the smiley face on
the front of a steampunk steamroller.
we have heard the ice cream truck at
midnight. take a bow, salute the vast
continents we drowned with liquid paper,
pine needles we mistook for hypodermics
(on the nod, even raindrops on bare skin
felt like unanswered emails from mom).
once i tried long-term investing: it was
like hunting an angel and finding a piano
when you're fresh out of fingers. is your
new meme laughing with me, or at me?
all-inclusive shuttle bus tour of disney's
purgatorio, salvation sold separately.
half-memory of a ghost stuck in a tree
was it real or only after-school tv?
you might think it would be easier by
now. easy as breathing blindfolded.
easy as waking up instead of down.

If I Was a Mountain

the shovel was old and the hole had no
bottom but there was two of us so the
dank infinity felt only half as big. 'normal'
was up on a shelf i just couldn't reach.
our accountant said something about
double jeopardy. we owed money but
i felt we were owed an explanation.
they stuck a band-aid on a slum and
declared victory; painted stone age
bible verses on space age bombs.
suburban verbs battled downtown
nouns: nestle and pepsi divided the
spoils, threw pretzels at the proles.
if i had a ladder i could see better. if
was a mountain maybe i could see
the middle class but so far they're
just a rumor. i did see a flamingo at
the zoo once—what a neck, what
cotton-candy crystal plumage! they
carved the wrong name on the dead
man's chest, opened a door that was
really a scar. nooses disguised as
novelty neckties, kardashian-flavored
bots at the bottom of the cereal box.

Super Big Gulp Migraine in the Multiverse Motel

stranger than ever but at least i'm always
me: it's the starring role i was born to play!
faces blurry in the rusty dusk, clinking
empties, and who invited billy bug-eyes,
scaring everyone with gory doomsday
scenarios, and why is he so gleeful?
bill, even after forever you'll never be the
hero; you'll be lucky to be the hero's
dirty sock. stop blaming the decepticons,
stop blaming dad. who needs a devil
when october bleaches the colors out
of the rose garden? when her plane was
loading i could have said *wait,* and didn't.
somewhere in the multiverse there's a
darkened stage with an audience of one
where i'm saying exactly what i mean
but so what, i can't get there, there's a
wall in my way. mountain-size migraine,
hollow-man sundays without any sun.
adulting entails being your own ghost: an
outsourced haunting just doesn't count.
have-not countries at the corners of the
map lose faith, fall right off the edge of
the world. it was only funny the first time.

When I Say Holy I Mean Temporary

suplex the day into smithereens, reassemble
it and wind up with a fistful of leftover parts.
somewhere a maple tree is missing an axle,
somewhere a toyota is wrestling a unicorn.
but it just felt right to trade the white house
for a barbie and ken dream home, my leaky
heart valve for a fatal antique metronome.
how embarrassing to fall in love with a
mountain, and not just for the mountain!
still better to have loved a ghost than to
play it safe and tag in the stunt man. but
that whole week in halifax i couldn't stop
remembering that week in disneyland.
you asked me where i really was; mickey
and minnie never stopped smiling. but
why did we have to wait so long for space
mountain? guess it doesn't matter now.
magical is my kingdom precisely because
it's temporary. watched a tiny piece of
information race from my big toe to a
neuron in my spine—before it got halfway,
civilization was out of gas. these days,
whenever i see someone not wearing
headphones i assume she's an angel.

Operation: Victory!

the gift left unopened turns into a curse.
a horn-shaped germ grows out of my
heart. it hurts, but pulling it out would
hurt worse. freeway murders forest,
eyeball swallows world, spotted tree
frog hits the panic button. a quark
howls, squirms on a strip of flypaper.
we marvel at the rates of exchange,
season the massacre with pumpkin
spice and call it 'operation: victory.'
dismembered bowling alley trophy;
pre-shrunk clouds, soaking in javex
bleach. old fridges and freezers,
pockmarked with bullet holes,
rotting in the post-mad-max dusk.
under sherman ave. there's a sacred
river, a legendary tributary, ancient
pulse of a great flood. the undertow's
magnetic, fatal. put down the phone.
behind the wall there's a book that
talks, a book with eight legs from a
kingdom without a name. beyond
the erotic pixel web, an older, wiser
alphabet, waiting just for you.

Confetti-Based Life Form

stub your toe and you're speed-dialing
a grief counselor. grizzly adams and
captain caveman would laugh at you,
your passive-aggressive email chains.
thought i'd discovered a new comet but
my telescope's not a telescope, just an
empty shot glass and it's not even dark
yet. if i ever name a comet i'll name it
dad, penance for all those pointless
arguments and scars. told him i wasn't
one of his better investments. by then
it was too late. it's always too late
somewhere. i inherited his rage and
gigantism of the spleen: no shortage
of sour bile at *this* mailing address!
zoom goes the day, zipping by on
roller blades. there were years i didn't
even breathe, years that got by just
fine without me. disposable datum
in a looney-bin choir: my spirit animal's
a bobblehead minion. everyone in
jeans, then everyone in hazmat suits.
can't believe i ever thought this
noose matched those shoes.

Geometry of Thunder

there was music, and tomahawk missiles
—brutal counter-offensives punctuated
the doo-wop and the bee-bop. i thought
of first kisses and the end of days,
whispered, *how ridiculous,* my wild
hungers, my voracious need to eat
my own scars until there's nothing
left, just some frantic graffiti on the
linoleum tiles in our old apartment.
geometry of thunder, lepidoptera
howling, swarming, then dying.
monday morning sneaks up on us,
wearing an undertaker's tuxedo.
goblins with gucci handbags—one
of them says, *we already ground
the redwoods into junk mail, so
what's a few rusty coins between
friends?* in the new economy
everybody is somebody else's
i.o.u. dumpster-fire algebra,
cardboard heroes glowing in the
walmart neon. native flora and
fauna, choking on toy soldiers.

Bloody Bulk Discount

as fluorescent halogen warms his cheek,
the getaway driver thinks of bills he can't
pay. there's a liquidity crisis in the bond
market, and scars on his back engraved
by a federal reserve board with rabies.
a good bender used to be almost free;
now i sell my blood until i faint and still
can't buy a laugh. one new year's eve,
martin wouldn't stop cartwheeling.
kid mix-up and lys were there, and
between life and death's the width
of a wall. weepy ash of the tinfoil:
we smoked that too. smoke was
everywhere that year, pooling in
our ear canals, choking the moss that
painted the rocks muppet-pillow-green.
less and less at home on the earth—
a disturbing trend! loneliness like a
demonic itch hounded me through the
raspberry bogs and shooting galleries,
the kosher deli with the broken sign.
once there was a street and a street
after that, and the corner of barton
and sherman doesn't owe us a thing.

Fossilized Triceratops Horn Retirement Plan

romeo takes the easy way out, leaves
juliet waiting at the station. goblins at
the farmer's market drive hard bargains.
plus and minus signs battle in the sky;
the billionaire offered us magnets for
miracles and we actually fell for it! a
super-big-gulp-shaped impact crater:
glowing ember of the bridge we burned.
how much greener grass could have
been if we hadn't fed the leviathan.
never should have played nice with the
cyclops, some kids you just can't reach.
but that's what they said about me
when it came to long division. math
always left a cruel taste in my mouth,
like when modal logic stole ifrah's
coral bracelet a decade after linear
algebra stole away ifrah. picture a
retirement plan carved out of minus
signs, and sandbags stuffed with sun-
bleached captain america dolls our
only barricade against tomorrow's
armies. shadow of an infinite zero,
soul reflected in an android's boot.

Clouds Catch Fire

maybe i could ask the geriatric rock star
community for a refund, or at least an
explanation. they were the kings of
over-promise and under-deliver, and
objects in the broken glass are weirder
than they appear. all those wasted years.
exile on stagflation street. billion dollar
maybe. slave of an outdated playbook,
lost samurai spinning his wheels in
cheektowaga's walden galleria mall.
my shadow, choking on the shadows
of microsoft windows 98, the y2k bug.
shadows kissing in the shadow of the
long-range hypersonic missile array:
lockheed martin's impact craters are
second to none! clouds catch fire,
rocks melt into weepy lava, marble
regresses to mute limestone. oh
erotic igneous ignition! oh mother!
melodrama's my soul's inherited
kink; every time i blink my eyes i
hear the sound of breaking glass.
moldy trophy memorial parade. stale
prayers tangled up in dead satellites.

Do-It-Yourself Cosmic Cube

autobots discover sentinel prime, frozen,
on the dark side of the moon, and my
favorite part of the movie is the popcorn,
her electric fingertips squirming in the
dark. decepticon wormhole bottleneck,
urgent clang of transformation, landlord
without a sense of humor. maybe i'll
think of something at the last minute,
invent a lucky charm, a cosmic cube. if
i knew the words i could slap handcuffs
on a soap bubble, explain a whole year
by explaining the sky they painted above
the switching station's barbed wire. in old
movies you can fix your problems by tap
dancing, stealing the mayor's daughter,
but now heaven smells like silly putty,
lightning bolts like chatbot styrofoam.
barter with the subprime lender, kick
a can of coke zero, wait for the echo.
chemtrails coded like squid scribble,
random light bulbs that remind her of
celluloid tragedies, godzilla jubilees.
she says glasses are always half full:
even when sleepwalking, i'm tripping.

Beginner's Guide to Forced Perspective

nobody who meets my heart's own riddle
thinks she's just a rowdy rodeo of atoms.
that's where her story begins, not ends.
looks like scientific american got it wrong
again. see bigfoot, see flying cars on mars.
there's a poem that keeps on flying apart
at the speed of light and i blame the usual
suspects: wicked magnets, poisoned rain,
rebel trajectory vectors of a secret math,
understudy of the kiss i always missed.
eternally unzipped, forever starting over.
synth-pop staccato of the red-bellied
woodpecker; rusty pliers that stand in
for crucifix in a pinch, in the rusty hinge
where ward 3 meets up-and-coming
ward 4. these electrons of mine sure
have seen a lot—some things we saw
didn't even have names! nouns always
let me down anyhow. like the one that
let her catch the montreal-toronto
shuttle bus when my tongue was
too thick to say sorry. zoom out and
it's a comedy. my tears feed the
aikido stance of tomorrow's fog.

After Hours Cryptogram

rope ladders hanging off the fire escapes,
lifesize headless monsters in the circle-k
windows and all i can think of is the sweet
spot where her clavicle and sternum meet—
o holy grail of my bumper-car hero's journey!
o is a letter in search of an o-shaped mouth.
home is a just rumor, forever out of reach.
it only gets dark a block-and-a-half at a
time and i suppose that's a kindness, a
lovely gesture from our all-new nickel-
plated metal gods. run straight home.
trust the news, even when it isn't new.
meanwhile, interstate 787 to albany
showed me a million ways to shed my
skin but no, it was just a trick, the real
me isn't going anywhere. in dreams
i try to explain it all to my kindergarten
classmates but they have horns, fins,
snakes in their hair and no time to spare.
sorry, we were talking about her clavicle?
she thrills me like a secret immortal bird:
smile carved out of song, algebra of her
braids like a world-eating algorithm.
even her small talk tastes like limes.

Sky Versus Sky

imagine fighting that hard over a *stapler*.
never heard you say a dirty word before,
and it's not like i waterboarded you, or
let it all burn down just for the lols. is
this really about the expired sour cream
at the back of the fridge? i can explain.
there once was a crooked man who read
too many books. he laughed at the wrong
times, battled with volkswagens like they
were lucifer's own dragons. thought he
was the lead when the credits listed him
as juror #6. a surprise witness appeared
at the last minute, casting all our basic
axioms into doubt. now even two plus
two is up for grabs. that's no puddle,
that's a teardrop. first time i've cried
since rocky 4. the screaming sky
claws at the roof. there's another sky,
bedazzled with white phosphorus
artillery shells, jellied gasoline sticky
as gummi bears. i apologize, the
stapler's all yours forever. later on,
ambassadors of the great source
will whisper to us in our dreams.

That's No Pixel, That's My Skull

so much heartbreak over one faulty map!
the riddle at the world's edge never came
any closer no matter how hard i tried.
old friends obsess over cholesterol,
binge watch doomsday prophecies,
gleeful as ghouls. funny to feel the
language we shared just slip away
like that. soon i'll have to light myself
on fire just to get the waiter's attention.
brought a hot air balloon to a gunfight,
kryptonite elves to the class reunion.
wound up with a pocket full of rain,
every throb of my heart a question-
mark-shaped howl. demons entered
the chat, made me doubt my name,
wonder if everything post-big-bang is
the grand hoax of a drunk dramaturge.
nate's passenger seat was just my size.
i loved watching the pines whip by the
window, holier than old cathedrals.
north america was one grand mystery:
occult slums of antimatter and wire,
poisoned roads scarecrow-stuffed
with crucial prehistoric mythologies.

Language of One

my mind's a perfect circle. i mean,
a zero, that nullifier of multipliers.
the wire that runs from my eye to
the world is haunted by a ghost
with a sick sense of humor. bad
puns, ninja stars in the crock pot,
that sort of thing. when i stare at
a rainbow until it's transmuted
into acres of economic integers,
that's him. sunshine beaming up
instead of down, that's him too.
every word a landmine—imagine
having to do a little dance, draw
a picture, because your nouns
were all being held for ransom.
let's talk more about nothing—
the last laugh, echoing through
the cave, your black lipstick,
staining my shirt, the red skull
smirking at our big screen epic.
all the girls used hairspray back
then. trees look so different than
trees on tv, and if this apple was
a grenade i swear i'd throw it.

Legendary Planetary Tango

thursday's borrowed majesty, my
brittle wish for something that won't
just dissolve when i lose faith in it.
the bouquet of your departure—
spooky as a dead man's suitcase.
next time give me a little warning;
some days just an eyeblink or two
without you has me reaching for
the lifeboats. so many screens
between my nouns and yours!
so many heart-shaped dead-end
streets since they changed the
national anthem to nails on a
chalkboard. let the madness be
your guide, your blinking check
engine soon light in the sacred
sky, out past the harvest moon.
it wasn't always so crowded up
there. stars drunkenly saluted
the ragwort, the runaways, all
the world's rowdy ligaments.
planets twirled like acrobats.
every atom had a story to tell.
you remember: you were there.

Melanie Misunderstood

i don't care what politician you endorse, but
for twenty dollars, i could pretend. that's
what we mean by 'social contract.' act like
you see me, not just who you
want to see, kiss me with pepper
spray but wash your hands first. this
meeting could have been an email.
find a magic marker, draw a face on
a balloon and call it darrell, i'd be
so grateful. i used to hit the panic
button over the littlest things! we'd
argue until our throats hurt, i was
sure i'd die if i didn't set the record
straight, about melanie and the
housewarming party, how they
all said it wasn't a big deal but
i knew it was. imagine a well
without a bottom, imagine a shoe
forever falling. or try carrying a
planet on your back–then you
can talk to me about big deals. i
stop to marvel at the fact of my
existence on the way to the doctor.
my rebel cells will just have to wait.

Mindful While Climbing

the war was boring and now it's night.
the day's cadaver twitches with fleas.
clocks are cruel and/or downright abusive,
i wish we instead marked our days with
schools of fish or glacially-slow cultures

of coral. never met a dial, a switch, or
an opposable thumb i could really trust,
and if bigfoot isn't real at least he never
lied to me about my career prospects,
the war in baghdad, the way terrorists
and freedom fighters switch costumes
during intermission. that was awkward:
the tongue-tied tomahawk missile, the
crimson blush of the impact crater.
regarding life i'm not a master or an
admiral. can't heal a broken pocket,
can't count up and down at the same
time, can't think about my thinking

if science says we're already history.
when i'm popular i know i'm dreaming.
there's a quest i slept on, a whole
generous battalion i forgot to thank.
i'm a stranger in my own biography,
betting it all on a rope made of sand.

Reversed Thunder

sami says, dna is and, backwards–what
do you think that means? i say nothing
means anything, meaning, nothing is
nothing is what's in my glass, hint hint.
sometimes you have to stare up at the
moon until the demon of desire relents.
up close the sun isn't a tomato, just like
earth isn't really a marble. the sun's a
storm that never ends, and emptiness
isn't really that empty. we tell tomorrow
not yet, hit pause so we can catch our
breath. after the riot squad swipes out,
goblins pick the pockets of the dead,
try to guess their bitcoin wallet logins.
is there money in the afterlife? doubt it.
money breeds in the dark, can't tell
jade from grenade, remains resolutely
allergic to me no matter how fervent
the prayer chain. guess i'll make do
without it, just like the silvery moon.
her light, its reflection, slipped right
through my fingers until i was empty
as a bubble and ready to start again.
my life spelled backward is a laugh.

Rules of Transit

a voice on speakerphone screams out
i would have gouged out my eyes for you!
and i am sorely tempted to tap the sign.
do not ask the bus driver for a loan.
zero tolerance for violence or melodrama.
and if love is a hoax, keep it to yourself.
in case of emergency, parachutes will
deploy automatically: no need to panic.
ease up on the pre-emptive stabbings.
i remember when we didn't need a sign.
everything—all nouns, their magnetic
fields—glittered like stained glass, city
blocks swaddled in a frosty enamel.
i dream of melting, like the light that
rinses the lawn and then disappears.
somewhere there's a cave with my
name on it, and who needs alphabets
when we are strangers to ourselves?
a blind woman clutches her baguette,
asks me for directions but my compass
always points towards thoughts of my
wife's flesh, the flesh i know best,
trembling and echoing my own. my true
north star: her wild undomesticated skin.

Obliteration Blizzard

a holy connection was bartered away: now
even a sunrise is just another screensaver.
someone's phone's ufo encounter is liked
by someone else's phone. thought i saw
jupiter, once, despite stelco's rusty dome,
but quickly talked myself out of it. surely
jupiter has more important places to be,
and i've been wrong before. there are
gradations of debauch, of sloth, roasted
ducks under glass. seems like everyone's
in a hurry except me. all i know of galaxies
is a reflection in a pond, and how can there
be so many stars, rutting and rocking in the
lazy current. silence shrinks the extremities.
this is the choose-your-own-adventure book
where the ferris wheel stops dead, leaving
you stranded and screaming at the top.
in church they said there's another world
inside every grain of sand, and we only
validate parking if you're a member. the
federal reserve says sorry about your luck.
should have planned ahead but where's
the fun in that? a joker without a joke: a
crazy-quilt world with a hollywood facelift.

Dandelion Logic

i know next to nothing about elderberries.
my own pollinators are perfect strangers.
i only think i have a heart, and not three,
because a mouth with a lab coat said so.
where does my body go when i'm asleep?
if i'm a sleepwalking bank robber, that
would explain the muddy footprints,
the suspiciously large e-transfers.
magneto bribed the jury, that's why he
only got probation after destroying a
billion dollars of real estate equity.
titanium man demands a raise, more
lines, a larger cut of the ticket sales. his
name in a larger font would be nice too.
remember the child prodigies who could
hold their breath until they levitated?
one of them generates nuclear codes,
another skims off the top of an ngo.
what's it like to be important? i asked
a pregnant dandelion head erupting
out of a flowerpot. no answer, unless
you count the way it kisses the sun
right before the seeds take flight.
there is a fire that never goes out.

Prisoners of Gravity

the local hysteria says vote early, vote often. an
eight-legged tumor on a leash hogs the sidewalk.
you can read entire libraries and learn nothing.
i slap random strangers to get my point across:
what else can i do when we don't even share
a grammar? zero is to hero as ladders are to
snakes, at least that's what i thought you said.
correct me if i'm wrong. is that howl radio waves
from a dead galaxy, or just a celebrity chef
looking for clicks? hydrogen's a cruel majority
up there, down here it's a rarity, and if i had a
kite, i would fly it. if i jump up and down long
enough, how would that impact the planet's
grip on the icy nothing? i ask because i miss
the moon 12 hours a day, dream of a celestial
reconciliation. maybe if we all do handstands
when the sun is directly overhead, the earth
will change gears, give mars a great big hug.
we'll recruit the tides, pray it's not a bummer,
like the night the night realized he's no knight,
he's just a character in someone else's book.
terror struck his heart: he'd rather be crazy
than imaginary. i think i know how he felt:
everything's alive and no one ever told me.

My Statement of Faith

buckthorn chokes a derelict house. i stare,
resist the urge to deliver a sermon on the
riotous machineries of joy. my personhood
is judged, then immediately forgotten, by a
dragonfly but that's ok; solid matter is just
frozen light and not as solid as you think.
my statement of faith is too iffy by half, like
dead branches piled by the curb, so naked
and nameless, who knows what starling,
what song, sheltered in their shade. and
all day a fiery river between us, echo of
the words i didn't say. i smell a clue,
chase it across ward 3, ward 2, then out
where the property values spike and
the chittering sprinklers glare at me
with disgust. i lived in a basement
around here, long ago, but fractional
reserve banking says a scrapbook's
just old papers, don't expect any
favors. dead souls wrapped in neon.
holy tree of memory, pulped into
junk mail. wookie-howl ringtone.
doomsday screensaver. dinosaur
hoof in a bucket of banana peels.

Mystery on the Endoscopy Express

if space is infinite, there's a galaxy
where you knew just what to say on
that blind date, another one where
i'm shaking hands with a hurricane.
some nights you can't sleep, so you
walk, and raccoon eyes look right
through you. in 1998, an amazon
called me 'unique.' her eyes were wide;
i thought i was halfway there. roaring
zombies of the past rise up, tell the
future what the score is. everyone
deserves a galaxy, a new moon
with a fancy ribbon. they tied me to
a chair, shoved a telescope down
my throat, saw a red-eyed howling
bigfoot headbutting my ribs. guess
that explains why i bruise so easily.
they asked if i had benefits, didn't
like my answer. out on the street, my
galaxy was still there, waiting for me.
i like the misty mornings, studded with
birds you can hear but can't quite see.
and i don't mind if it's all just a dream:
landing is the price you pay for flying.

Wicked World Weld

the lead hand swings his mighty chain.
an old flame is renovicted by metrolinx,
a state monopoly with a mean streak.
fighting them is like holding back the
dusk with a celery stick, and how can
nights can be so long when life is so
short. cough cough—the air's thick with
iron dust from all the flex-cor welding.
a cancerous haze blinds the eye like
an ancestral hate. something funny
about spending 18 years feeding a
spool of wire into a flame, watching
its head ignite, morph into slag ash.
some men feed the fire until it's time
to choose a coffin. i want headroom.
firm pillows. an ice cube dispenser.
if this world isn't made for me, maybe
the next one is. ifrah is gone: one
less pension plan liability. tappayers
cheer but not me, such a mean math
that calls a loss a win. the ice cream
melted, dripped onto her jeans, she
laughed, and if i could have hit the
pause button forever, i would have.

Noonday Sun Eclipsed by a Pizza

i was out of rhymes, out of luck, so the spider
and i took turns giving each other piggyback
rides. to nurse a friend is to build a tower, to fail
is divine which means i'm 98% angel by now.
mammal brain begged reptile brain for a rematch,
a best-two-out-three. dodged the check so many
times my landlord called me the invisible man.
a local artist meditated on the sidewalk, sold
fingerpainted postcards of the weekly drone
strike. a fresh big bang lurked around every
corner. the state sold us an old crisis with a
fresh coat of paint, free oreos for early-bird
compliance, oreo crumble on the i-v drip for
the platinum-plated champion of the month.
what if the super-voter met the gladiator in
the arena and refused to fight, offered him
flowers instead of deadly knife wounds?
what if that scream was a bell, a magical
bell that rewound the world back to zero?
we could play house, beget a dynasty, i'd
dance backward all night if that's what it took.
a frenzy like heat lightning, your forgiveness,
and everything mattered like we were the
last lovers left alive, draped in flame.

Electron Carnival

some days even the right angles look wrong.
a reaper drone fired a sidewinder missile on
our behalf, there was nothing we could do
about it, we didn't even know why the sky is
blue, not really, something about a prism,
and among wavelengths there are winners
and losers but don't ask me for any details.
at low tide we found a boulder we adored,
we rested, kissed it, we didn't say a word.
nor did we count the minutes, lost forever
like ashes in the ocean, like sweet dreams
melting in the alarm clock's howl. what if i
staple together a fistful of maple leaves
and call it a book, and what if i hold my
breath until all the machine guns morph
into fun-filled confetti cannons? i didn't
ask that out loud, there was no need, she
understood, the surf's clickety-clack was
so eloquent it built a bridge between the
world and my mind's-eye view of it.
somewhere a blowtorch was singing.
somewhere a child was losing a tooth.
just a holy packet of time, without ribbons.
ever wonder where we'd be without them?

Casket of Crisis

a disaster postmarked for ohio wound up in
east lansing, the shooter's manifesto went
straight to the landfill, and my co-worker
won't shut up about how he used to be a
big shot, lost it all in a dot-com bubble. he
planted trees out west, changed his name,
saved his soul, then lost it again when his
luck changed. the abbot told him *maybe the
monastery isn't a good fit for you* so now
he's my problem. i wish the lunch room
was bigger. there's something tragic
about how the riggers and lead hands
line up and swipe out–even their dreams
are full of pulleys and winches, cables
and chains. my mouth is dry and on tv
a preacher is crying for all the lost souls,
his toll-free number blinks, he accepts
all major credit cards. hope the future
doesn't judge us too harshly. geologic
layer made of crippled action figures;
tropical biosphere sacrificed for crypto;
monuments overgrown with ivy. every
day's a burnt offering to some god or other.
try to pick the one with a sense of humor.

Snow Globe Locomotive Choo-choo

this new batch of heroes is a profound anticlimax.
fight the power, boycott the factory, save the
meme of the ant lugging a leaf ten times his
size—no hall of fame, no horny glory, and yet
our whole snow globe locomotive couldn't
choo-choo without it. and that last-minute
switcheroo was like a magic trick nobody
asked for. never should have looked the
carnival barker in the eye. never should
have thought that mom would live forever.
so many bolts and unused hex keys left
over after we built the cyclops, burned the
rice, begged for scraps from the subprime
lender. lost-and-found bric-a-brac adding
up to a masterpiece's identical twin, but
here's the thing about abstract art, here's
the thing about pain. crown point east has
been written off by three different levels of
government, surely we deserve some sort
of prize. hollow victories are my specialty.
hidden cameras watch me watch the world
fall apart and as a taxpayer i'm outraged.
i wanted the truth, they made false claims,
and even the spiderwebs feel like chains.

Secret Identity Written on Water

that flat tire in the rain, my lack of coping skills,
if i'd kept my cool, a golden highway like a
divine monopoly board would have unfurled
before us. if i bring home a stolen flower, will
that balance the scales? and if banyan trees
can homestead for free inside the temple
in the jungle, why do i have to pay rent?
but math was never my thing, after 2 x 2
i spaced out, couldn't wait to crawl out the
window before the world passed me by.
out there was a kingdom without a king, a

girl with opium tea and a red barrette. we
watched fireworks on the roof, wondered
if the future would be awful or awesome.
erosion erased a footprint of a blueprint.
lame, how staplers come with instructions
but a century doesn't. and what about
wings? so many systems updates i never
asked for and still no wings. with wings
my boss would never see me again, trust
me. having cloud towers under your feet
changes your whole attitude. nothing but
the best will do when you're lighter than air.
every spin a winner; every tooth a diamond.

Skeleton on a Treadmill

a knight kills a dragon, returns home to find the
locks have been changed. romee wrote
an epic letter but it never got sent. juliet said
no kisses before a thorough credit check
and three work-related references. at least
the seasons—the battle-scarred glory of their
comings and goings—never let us down,
staying forever beyond the ghoulish grasp
of richie rich. picture an hour that resembles syn
a skeleton on a treadmill, or the old-world
magic that carries the world on its back,
gone on strike. most of my thoughts can't
touch their own toes, let alone rescue the
princess. in dreams she's a castle full of
endless hallways, escape rooms of manifold
geometries. i wake up in the bath tub with my
pajamas on backward, shave an old man's
mask but my fingerprint still wants to party.
we try to feel the heat of as many stars as
possible but ifrah is still gone. she had a
favorite color but i never asked, and a
secret cave in a neural net as the repo
man stalked our soap bubble dream home.
the tylenol burns so bright it hurts my eyes.

Drowning in the Shallow End

my tax returns, and the ghost i carved in the
snow, are an epic ballad in shorthand, a
stuttering hero's journey from couch to coffin.
memories of the minute hand and the wrapper
they came in, and i am my own agonized
antagonist. all i can do is stuff wrenches
into the devil's cogs and gears until monday
blows a fuse. there's a bird that goes for years
without ever touching the ground and vulgar
epitaphs carved on obsolete dvd players; a
spider that celebrates being born by eating
its parents, and dead dogs in dead satellites
orbiting the rust belt. some particles leave
before they arrive with barely a la-di-da,
that's the trouble with making long term
plans. they said faster than light travel was
off the table but when it comes to popping
birthday balloons i know a short cut. learn
to walk before you try to swim: not all those
piranha are plastic. if a shark asks you for
i.d., look him in the eye and dance. if he
starts to blush, you're home free. if only
that cave man hadn't picked up that rock!
if only we still used our faces as currency.

Song of the Laughing Gorilla

no matter how many translations i try, it always ends
the same: the palace in flames, blood on
the world's grand piston. a caterpillar evades
predators by pretending to be a stick and i
pretend to be good. can't believe i lost faith
in the tightrope when i was half way across.
teddy bear in a coma, crib recycled into
firewood. lives fueled by colors, sabotaged
by numbers, and the way time ripped the
rings right off my fingers. whose dream is
really steering the ship? plastic novelty
eyeball, or earth seen from the moon?
afterlife's echo in the beforetime, or a
demon's hoofprints on the shag carpet?
if i rub my belly three times and dive
down the staircase, would it matter
at all to our stone-faced overlords? it's
a wonder more chairs don't go flying
out of motel windows. theme songs for
sugary snacks claw at our door, regroup,
skitter along the roof. with every swipe
of your debit card, somewhere a gorilla
is laughing at you. you, your prison
without walls, your furious halo of flies.

Aku Aku Sailboat in the Sky

found a heart on the beach at low tide, held
it up to my ear and heard the song of an
ancient army. implicit in the melody was
a fatal doom but a song that doesn't end
is no song at all, just static on a dead line.
in this precarious economy, a suicide puts a
tumor on the unemployment line so put the
gun down, try a different name in a different
town. never thought about death at all until
it happened to me. if i had a tail i'd wag it
all day, if i had a magic mirror i'd start over,
no mistakes this time, no more haggling
with the wizard. inside my cranium there's
a telescope full of stars, and a letting go
that's stronger than gravity. in my pocket
there are two rocks: one says yes, one
says no. a cave man said ooga booga
and explained more than i can with a
wheelbarrow full of dictionaries. my week
beats your year but some hours last a
lifetime. poured myself into a manifesto
but it was like a prayer without a motor.
spent passover under the overpass
and nobody got the joke but me.

Psalm Spasm

neutrinos are always passing through my
secret parts, that's why i sweat, that's why
the milk soured so fast. still, this twig is
magnificent, and with a face like that, this
blizzard should be a supermodel. ancient
celestial collisions spin me right round, yet
i pretend this excel spreadsheet matters.
objects in the mirror are weirder than they
appear, and i am wreck-racked with
spasms of psalms, detuned strummings
of spirographing comets, happy-faced
orbits reflecting off chrome bumpers.
words bloom, then bleed. letters
break formation, my mouth bites down
on air. every day we wander just to make
sure we're lost. dorothee says *remember
when they filmed a movie here, i thought
i saw a movie star but i couldn't be sure.*
the cop was out for justice, assassins lit
his car on fire, all night long our window
was full of flames. we watched dancing
lights bleed through the curtain, called
it all *enlightenment.* dorothee's kiss
tasted like a color without a name.

Dead Man's Float

the doctor uses words i don't understand. if i
caught the gist of it, my body is made out of
glass bottles that yearn to revert back into
sand, the blu-ray glare hurts their eyes, and the
way i second-guess even my grocery list makes
them pray for world war three. i ask for a
second opinion, he says the sun
is growing colder, i say that's not what i
meant, but i haven't meant what i said since
the 80's. now that was a decade that made
sense: this new stagflation leaves us with
nothing concrete enough to push against.
even sidewalks feel like sponges, granite
precambrian shelves trusty as trampolines.
if this dolphin had thumbs i bet he'd light the
fuse on the doomsday bomb himself, just
for a change of scenery. if i had fins, late fees
wouldn't matter. *matter* would hardy matter,
drifting weightlessly in my underwater world.
i'm less buoyant than a raft but too poor to be
worth kidnapping so i give myself a blue
check mark. there's always a grateful-inducing
giving and taking, even as the clock keeps
screaming like a meteor aimed at my heart.

When it Comes to Welding I'm No Einstein

the day starts wrong: i cancel the appointment.
i don't need a professional to tell me i should
have chosen the genie's lamp instead of the
bachelor's degree back when i was drunk on
hope and the internent had a nerds-only sign
slung over the front gate. hit snooze, pretend
that last x-ray was a paper airplane. dorothee
talks in her sleep with the urgency of a thriller
(the mission's always impossible, the time is
always now). i press against her, inhale like a
lovesick balloon: even in the heart of the city,
her hair smells like a pristine pine forest. how
i love her semi-waterproof skin-bag, the way
she peels onions and how she absorbs bad
news without unraveling. i knew a guy who
tore himself to pieces when an electric eye
made his life's work obsolete, another guy
who bet on the wrong unicorn and never
recovered. i think it's weird whenever i see
a house that *isn't* haunted, or a seatbelt that
doesn't rise up and strangle the electric ape
frantically adjusting the windshield wipers.
her eyelids flicker as the dream plot thickens.
today my head is stuffed with stale blizzards.

Marionette of Distant Stars

every man needs a project so i dedicate
myself to staring at lake erie, the horizon,
the neutral zone where the two blues meet.
stare long enough and shapes emerge:
roman war chariots, aeronautical ceo's
hanging off ledges, promises that felt so
permanent, defensive strategies melting
into punchlines. a face that says i *know
you are but what am i,* or a stick-man
pantomime of a soul's degradation.
next they'll be asking me what the
meaning of 'is' is. let's say you use
your capital and someone else's
capital to make more capital. the
numbers add up; your face is hot
with lust. soon you're picking fights,
dropping plates, the bank won't even
give you a free pen until you're back
where you started, but even the
moon is different now, slightly sour,
and her light feels artificial. i'm not
talking about me. try to focus. the
tide is rising. o beauty, so brutal
and wise, let me be your minion.

Sunset Chasing a Sunset

some days i feel like that doomsday prophet
who spent three days with a whale in his
stomach: zoom in and the prankmonkey's
quilting an artificial heart; zoom out and
abstraction rules the day, steers the cosmos.
the future's a burglar we passed on the stairs.
we hold our breath, avoid eye contact, hope
he's here to raid someone else's piggybank.
like midges attacking a screen door, a gentle
joy swarms the great wall of lonely, doesn't
replace it. objects and their adjectives wear
fancy scarves. itineraries like strange loops,
folded into blooms. like a thorn in the aorta
it still hurts when it rains, that slow-motion
memory of being picked dead last by the
team captain. my shadow self is like the
idea of a sunset chasing a sunset. smother
of peppermint and soldered slag: lonely
ricochet bouncing inside an empty skull.
the dream of a dial you forgot to twist,
silent-movie princess dancing on a raft.
strange, the way i remember places i
never visited. buried under the plastic
lawn, another life, familiar as my own.

Scatterization Cauterization

in my mind i can still see the hanging tree,
silhouetted against the ripe-tomato-sunset.
later, the vigilantes joined a secret society.
when i awake, i'm on the wrong side of a
standard deviation. juggling my revenge
fantasies is like playing ping pong with an
egg. hard to believe old yearbooks could
be so flammable. some days i wish i was
as cold as a stethoscope. a cell phone's
computing power is unburdened by
conscience–that's a powerful advantage
unless today's judgment day. but today's
monday and the garden of forking paths
is sprouting false positives in every
possible direction. some impossible
ones, too. there's foreign geometries,
alien logics and if you kissed me you'd
be kissing the me i used to be. i lie to
my dentist about how often i brush–the
one constant element in my life, a way
of keeping faith with my six-year-old
self. hope he's not too disappointed.
hope the bills aren't counterfeit, and the
getaway car is right where we left it.

Wings Mean Victory

she snores when she sleeps on her back, on
her side not at all. i treasure this data with
glee, gleeful as scrooge mcduck diving
into his swimming pool full of gold coins.
i swear i'll change, lean into the good, but
forget, waste a year marveling at fir trees.
at least nobody got hurt, as far as i know.
crying in the bathtub in a holiday inn out
west (tv exposions leaking through the wall)
i thought of runaway kids encountering
love and grief for the first time, trembled
at all the ridiculousness and waste we
never budgeted for—am i remembering,
or just imagining? there's another memory,
you know the one, like an abscessed molar
you just can't stop licking, the one where
she says we're all guilty of murder, even
if we're only talking about caterpillars and
midges ground into the heels of our nikes.
nike's wings mean victory but my nikes were
made by slaves so we change the subject,
argue sequels and prequels, and the way
time's a circle, everything returns, and up's
just a bad joke when you're this far down.

Ocean in an Eye Socket

it makes no sense to pretend to be normal or a
hummingbird with cement feathers when
deep down i'm still just a shaved gorilla;
with quicksand this sticky, my problems
ride piggyback on me wherever i go, like
a snail slugging his house on his back.
that left glove is either lost or stolen,
and the dead clock in the pharmacy at
barton and leinster always says 3:45.
ifrah battled a blizzard to get there but
they told her she had the wrong forms.
she said i had 'barton street eyes,'
she had problems i couldn't solve,
the demon was so oily my hardest
punches just slid right off him. haunted
houses are more my speed, haunted
buicks, haunted pool halls, failed
messiahs, feral cats that plop dead
birds right on my doorstep. why is the
way home always uphill, and the top
of the ladder just another square one
in someone else's rearview mirror?
there's a legend she liked, about curses
lifted, and about old wounds, redeemed.

Mechanoptera Borealis

the mystery remains resolutely unsolved.
maybe the murder weapon was an icicle
that melted just before the cops arrived,
maybe there's a crucial color we can't see.
atomic chains held together by paperclips,
the parking stub that was once a redwood,
the barcodes on the necks of the starving.
and how a news anchor's upspeak makes
me doubt her sincerity, reminds me of an
uncle, lost at sea, raging against the fates,
the chasm between us ever vaster like a
bad magic. i'd like to shake his hand,
listen to his favorite song. back then i'd
black out, have legendary exploits, have
to take the bouncer's word for it. what if
the meaning of life is a spot on a ladybug's
back? why does life have to mean anything;
why can't it just be lovely, like a garden?
and did you mean it when you called me a
sinner, or were you just saying what you
thought the algorithm wanted to hear?
let one rowdy variable stay out late and
poof, everything's up for grabs. galaxy-
sized gash. cranium full of dead leaves.

Sky Battery Puppet Show

all my dance moves, the riddles i carved
into endangered trees, express a deadly
seriousness like a scarecrow stuffed with
grenades. shadows of tongue and talon,
melody of lava like an earworm in the
waiting room. cheap happy endings
laugh into their sleeves, they always
knew nothing ever ends, and there's
always a wheelbarrow full of banana
peels just waiting to collide into our
blue-chip nest egg. daisy chains of
disaster crowd the subway platform,
every commuter an uneasy aggregate
of android-eyed spare parts. light is
still a mystery, i don't care what science
says. o giant battery in the sky, forgive
me for all of your heat i wasted. she
cracks walnuts, i crack jokes, and as
long as we don't say the word, the war
stays on the other side of the window.
sometimes i think about ancient rome,
old movie sets rusting in the desert.
and how even if the heart is grade-a,
some transplants just don't work out.

Breeze Carved Out of Quicksand

how odd it is to wake up in this bus shelter
instead of another. how odd it is to wake up.
now what? the cafe is full of stormtroopers
chomping on donut holes, maybe i'll skip it.
where do they find so much confidence?
maybe it comes with the uniform. the fish
we laugh at for not knowing water is wet
laugh at us for not knowing air is stuffed
with the sad ghosts of our first date kisses.
between us there's a graveyard of broken
triangles and even breezes are carved out
of quicksand. think of a lake turned inside
out, or a circle that's all thumbs. invisible
trap doors knitted together with stolen wire:
that's what we've been swimming through,
that explains all these tears, those footnotes
blaming war crimes on a rough childhood.
old movies feature cameos from ex-lovers,
ex-landlords, while the intersection of gage
and barton is full of dead stars, legendary
monsters. that's no drum, that's my heart.
a sad-eyed water droplet spies for the man.
inside every mammal's a reptile on a tricycle.
even my blanket comes with a warning label.

The Only Game in Town

martin thinks he's just a head in a jar
but if he's right, what would change?
rules would still have to be followed.
one death per ticket: no exceptions.
it can be loud as a cloud or as subtle
as a high-five from the invisible man.
the venus flytrap starts to scream,
the riprap of the bathtub's drip is
brother to noah's great flood, and
after the restructuring these too-
bright sunrises hit like hammers.
lego baby yoda smiles up from
the knife drawer. who let him in
here? have or have not, he tells
me, there is no why. the giants
play rough, they cut our ties to
the old ways, the old erotic dirt.
i cried for a week after the bride
of frankenstein flipped the switch.
there's a patchwork meat-man,
born in a storm, inside all of us.
there's a time for thinking and that
time is not now. if the world's an
illusion it's still my favorite one.

Memory of a Memory

out of reach, even out of sight, lightning
ignites the air, cracks the night's dome
wide open, and lightning is something
that only happens in the past. reminds
me of seeing ifrah at the corners of gage
and barton, gage and cannon, years
after she joined the sorority of ghosts.
back then there were birds, kingfishers
too many to count, i asked strangers
if the flock numbered odd or even,
desperate for a mathematical proof i
could sink my teeth into, some divine
axiom sturdy as the world's own axis.
ice cream cone crushed by bulldozer,
nuclear sub circling the toilet bowl,
and everybody sheds their skin but
only in yesterday, that's where heroic
fiascos belong. maybe tomorrow
will be different. the security guard
could have a sense of humor, the
sabretooth tiger a full stomach.
the heart needs its fangs like the
river needs a song. did we ask for
too much or not quite enough?

Mathemagica

every day more of me resides in the past, the
fatal slippage mainly unnoticed like a sneaky
pancreatic tumor dodging the x-ray. inhaled
more metal than air at national steel car,
staring down the blowtorch's white-hot
wire. always felt guilty on payday: i'd
promised heaven that if i got the job, i'd do
something about those starving children
that haunted late night cable, then just
never got around to it. rocks
cry out, but only other rocks can hear.
war remained on the other side of the
window, and cowboy gunfights in front
of the mirror don't count for much when
whiz kids on scholarships make our
death stars ever more user-friendly
and cost-effective. numbers don't lie?
sure they do. bipeds have just had more
practice. you talk in your sleep, i write
the words down, guard my notebook
like it's houdini's own skeleton key.
oily spools of time i should have
preserved in mom's old canning jars.
ancient anthems, all just static now.

Love Letter Lost in the Mail

night, again? didn't we just say goodbye?
take your best shot, you cruel calculus!
that last punch didn't even hurt, and
solid stone is just cotton candy to a
fast enough road runner. that's just
science. a flash from a distant star,
frying our telemetry, is an erotic dm
intended for the old jurassic lizards.
nasa eavesdrops, doesn't even blush.
we put price tags on water, don't even
blush. dinosaur dead letter office.
a memory, slippery as money. a
warhead, delivered by uber eats.
magnesium flash behind the eye.
bad karma gumming up the motor,
like newton's first law of paying
your dues. never saw leo offer
to pick up the check. montreal,
last i heard, stealing copper from
victorian row houses and trading
crypto. what castle should i storm
when our fall from heaven is all
cgi greenscreen? must be real
magic around here somewhere.

Fathers in Cheap Motels

now that war fever is back in bloom,
every day i want to feed the ducks.
now that we've lost our hotline to the
parliaments of the air, quack quack
is what i say. my vote matters?
quack. we appreciate your business?
quack. time's a hammer looking for a
nail. born-again-too-late dream, salty
aftertaste of a life less domesticated.
pieta with track marks in the hall of
justice parking lot; pencil crayon sos
obliterated by rain. how frantically
we memorize the last minute script
changes. the killer's a werewolf now,
and daddy won't be coming home. he
stares at the flag on the motel room
wall. he doesn't reach for an ax; his
rage twists inward, feasts on pain
and blood. how he hated his dad;
how he stole his dad's every move.
the grace of it resides in the thunder,
telling us even the sky has a boss,
even the day has a cast-iron lid. then,
a long-distance call, a wild light—

World War Wasp

a wasp lands on my cereal bowl.
i challenge him to a staring contest:
he agrees. time flies and we form a
bond: we are both parts of a whole,
baffled by the world, baffled by the
other. reflected in his google of eyes
i'm ashamed of my simian self, my
wormy fingers, sneaky as a clock
in a dream. there's a lesson here.
now it's years later. i'm old. i'm not
sure if this is the same wasp or one
of his descendants. we both can't
believe they're still making bombs,
and making babies beg for water
because of luckless geography and
an end-times prophecy. maybe we
should thank wasp world for never
sowing main street with land mines,
and no spider ever lied to me about
where money comes from. primates
have earned themselves a time out.
imagine having 5 eyes like a wasp,
seeing life as a cathedral carved
out of stained-glass telescopes.

Modern Prototype Foundry and Castings

inside my head's a picture of a house
and inside that house is where i live.
weird that paper and liquid paper don't
repel each other like misaligned magnets.
weird that every head thinks every other
head holds a life-giving secret, but there
is no secret, and if you want the window
seat, i won't fight over it. you stole a
leather jacket that wasn't even your size,
asked how fast you'd have to cartwheel
to spontaneously combust, i apologized,
said that's just not how friction works.
nobody else ever called me poindexter.
you remind me of something, but not
u.s. steel, not the mill where i always
wound up with the wrong sized wrench.
in the lunchroom lifers snorted powder
off rough plywood sheets, gagged,
said, 'wives, you know what i mean?'
when the temp agency said i wasn't
a good fit, i didn't argue. whatever job
i ever had or lost, the moon was always
there for me, following me home
like a great impossible wisdom.

Hurricane Quixote

what good's a grammar when the words
don't fit, and vandals have stripped the
time machine of all its copper? after
hurricane quixote there were so many
oldsmobiles at the bottom of the canal,
catfish and beavers threatened a strike:
if the natural world ever got organized,
homo sapiens wouldn't have a chance.
picture a soul. now picture a soul
without a transmission, suspended
on cement blocks, mutely corroding
under a nike swish of neutron stars.
never did figure out how mirrors work. if
i did i'd dive right in, leave myself behind.
that's no scarf that's a snake, actually
it's the rope of sand i called a career.
maybe asking if bodies are shadows of
spirits is what cost me that promotion.
the invention of alphabets has proven
to be a mixed bag. strange duet of eye
and weather pattern. half-spun web of
thistle, furious jibber-jabber of cicadas.
i read a book that said there are other
worlds but this is the only one for me.

Algebracadabra

you told her you'd die without her and you
were right, you *did* die, every morning,
for years. bits of you flaked off like spools
of abandoned snakeskin. old songs in
balcony windows took on new meanings.
never again to argue over up or down.
the ice cube screams, cracks right in two.
swimming pools choke on dead leaves;
the jury is ready to render its verdict.
drumroll as you tap on your turn signal,
canned laughter as you miss your shot.
husbands ask other husbands for tips;
some spell out morse code distress
signals with eye blinks like prisoners
of war. life can flash by if you let it; that's
why i didn't sleep from summer of '97 to
spring of '98. not an unqualified success
but i think i deserve an 'a' for effort.
zigzag zoom of a hero's tragic journey,
stormbringer with a migraine, goddess of
death juggling matches and lighter fluid.
and all because of a minus sign instead
of a plus sign, and a butterfly far away. i
study my scars like roadmaps to the stars.

Scream's-Eye-View

if the howl of your hands lays bear traps
out for the song of your heart, you may
already be a winner. what's so special
about a unicorn, just a horse with a
hood ornament, but i'm sure if i could
afford one i would change my story.
a maple key circling a storm drain
suits my budget much better. the
coding scripts that went obsolete
while i was busy staring at trees!
how many times we almost started
world war 3 because of a radar
blip sparked by a flock of geese!
your connection is freezing up.
try rinsing your iphone in lava
and putting your foot through the
kitchen window. i've seen it work.
here's the problem: your settings
are still set for hunter-gatherer.
and lose the vestigial tail. rowdy
rebel voltage, melody with a tumor,
dragonfly screaming on flypaper.
roar of the eyelid, slamming shut.
drunken moon, dancing on a wire.

Scab Song

can a civilization be glued together with
python blood and python code while
juggling doll parts and spent shell casings?
something tells me we're about to find out.
a dream so vivid it makes me scream, a
fatal geometry that worked so well on paper.
they pay me to make the hard decisions,
says the lunatic as he gives the bombers
the green light. landmines in the lunch box,
swampy gunk of private purgatories. i
turn away, marvel at the way the scab
drapes itself over the wound like a
favorite blanket. maybe english isn't for
me, i bark like a dog at the bark of a tree,
tell the lepidoptera family to hold my calls.
there's a truth i just can't carry, a pixilated
blur right where the halo should be. i'm
comforted now by smaller mythologies,
scraped off the bottom of the bargain bin.
i write love letters to the birds i heard but
never saw, fold them into paper planes,
launch them off the balcony. hawthorn
branch like a hitchhiker's thumb; family
hex that boomerangs back, redeemed.

Credit Limit Increase Denied

the plan was to grow horns. the plan was,
when the darkness, tiptoeing like a thief,
swallows your lover, become the darkness.
if i had to choose between existence and
essence, i'd probably pick a strawberry.
when you said i don't care i said of course
i care, but only in an oblique sort of way,
the way an amoeba cares about a buick.
i dream of final exams, i dream we're
by the canal and i can look but not touch.
how odd to win a free play on a scratch
card, step out of 7-11 and lock eyes with
an owl, right in the middle of downtown!
the adult eastern screech owl weighs

160 grams and never broke my heart.
bird shadow slams into the bank of america
with a boom so loud, my teeth feel loose.
i'm on the outside, looking in, not even
offered the complimentary calendar.
grand mal seizure, or seizure of assets?
in my case, the answer is yes and yes.
neuron ion sweet as an oreo sundae.
ten pounds of lust in a 5 pound bag.
rented soul, hollow as a snare drum.

Dear America

just saw an old roommate in a youtube ad,
offering his services as a life coach.
mindfulness is his specialty now. when i
knew him, he would bang his head into
the drywall, all night long, just for the
bragging rights. funny, how time bends.
econoline van up on blocks, shedding
iron oxide atoms like unheard prayers.
rocky mountain, ground into powder.
a grand melody with ancient meaning
drowned out by the howl of dofasco's
electric arc furnace. putting a happy
face sticker on the biopsy didn't help.
i don't know what the oncologist was
thinking. there's a face in the sky. his
lips move but i don't hear a sound.
dear america, throw a dreamweb all
over our zigzag busywork, make it
add up something more permanent,
some epitaph sturdier than a spider
web, the candy wrappers the apollo
astronauts left behind on the moon,
the bloody bite marks my teeth
chiseled into dorothee's heart.

New Recruit Distracted by Fireflies

caffeinated staccato. light unfurls, congeals
into pools, glides across the lawn. it wasn't
dead, only sleeping. fireflies are another
story. all night i watched them headbutt
the air, headbutt each other, headbutt
the ancient chestnuts and oaks. i felt
the absence of any anchor, without the
words for what i felt. somewhere there
were murders, never to be solved, big
shots gobbling up the future, and a
soul without a why or how is like a hot
air balloon without the hot air. code a
missile launch, pass through fire,
beat the unbeatable tetris level–
that's a lot of hoops to jump through
for an unpaid internship. i didn't say
ok boomer or ask him how he slept
at night, but another past due notice
and i'll be selling a kidney. figments
of someone else's imagination,
fragile as a flower's daydream of
a limestone escarpment, dea
ocean's skeleton-song. analog
antenna in a world gone digital.

Flower-Star Staredown

heavenly bodies and earthbound flora stare
lustily at each other in a drunken
communion on different frequencies—
who even notices the promethean
chains of their love? bewilderment
like a ghost-thin spider web tickling
your face, like the new cereal aisle
where there's so many choices,
we just can't seem to choose. bet
if i held my breath for an hour i'd
see some changes around here.
to fill the ancient potholes on barton,
drastic measures may be required.
some butterflies pop into existence
uncaused, powered by private jokes.
anyone here tonight from out of town?
anyone here remember the cold war?
what do you say when you come *this*
close to world war 3 over a flock of
geese on a radar screen? sorry? but
that's what i said when i stayed out
late and dorothee stayed up all night
worrying. she said it was no big deal,
and even now, years later, i wonder.

Elephant-Sized Rubber Ducky

the soldier in the corner of the masterpiece
never knew that goya made him famous. the
painting has a hidden message but so does
this brick, and am i the dreamer or the dream?
a specialist told me to think of life as one long
exhalation, i asked him about his refund policy.
another suggested i ease up on accepting so
many invitations to secret societies but i've
always had a hard time saying no, no to wrong
numbers, no to parades passing by my window.
where do i sign, pied piper in a skeleton mask
i'm all yours. is the world broken or just bent?
found a hex in my soup, the waiter said he'd
heard that joke before. the other patrons licked
their plates clean, then licked each other. looked
for the exits, they'd been bricked over, smashed
through a wall wile e. coyote-style, promised
myself tomorrow will be different, haven't really
believed that since kindergarten. but even cruel
bureaucracies can wilt into dust when love's

queen bee lights the fuse. should our eyes
open and meet, our hearts high-five and grow
fins, what a glorious pandemonium that would
be! enough to make even the big bang jealous.

National Mechagodzilla Cartwheel Emergency

my worries are of the silly sort—looney-bin
easter pageants, faded record sleeves and
second skins i left behind with various exes.
scrape off the day's mascara, unhook my wings
of tinfoil, stare at the flipped piece of real estate
where thunder alley bowling lanes used to stand:
nothing much happens. the sky churns out vast
cinemascope ragnaroks—golden age regrets,
licking their wounds; demon robot watchdogs.
some days reality's all bark and no bite, a
papier mache tiger, a moon in the gutter. this
is my belief. if you don't like, i have others.
even after lengthy explanations and requisite
peace offerings, my wetware views my body
as a ruthless predatory interloper. that explains
why i fell out of bed without a life jacket,
apologizing to the shiver of sharks in the sink.
but who gave them the keys in the first place?
experience is a hard teacher, said the goldfish
bowl i brought to the knife fight. sunsets are
special when mechagodzilla is stomping on
your landlord. there's a bridge we forgot to
cross, and a future waiting for a fuse. this is
not a good time for cartwheels? the hell it isn't.

Inside the Outside

and remember how we tried to will ourselves
into weightlessness, just to see if we could
hike through the sand without leaving any
footprints? the lens of memory makes it all
seem super-heroic but gravity and time
get the last word. birds, out of pure spite,
spin a nest in the hair of the tightrope walker,
suspended over two moments, a churning
whirlpool far below. elon's ray gun carved
a scream-shaped hole right through a vast
school of plankton: a moment of silence
might be in order. here, there, don't care
where, just wake me up when ai can make
a crocus bloom, or save a soul in the budget
motel where you rent rooms by the hour.
picture a day so twisted, inside and outside
trade places; a sentence like a centipede,
so long that night for the head is day for the
tail. words like wet matches, words stuffed
into the suitcase i carried from zip code to
zip code. unnoticed, a man on fire walks
right by the doomscrollers. and what were the
larks gossiping about, right before i arrived? o
vast wordless endless: let me join your team.

Portable Singularity

she was my former friend's former soulmate.
not my best idea but not my worst, either. i
wish i could forget about acid-wash jeans,
uneasy mullets and noxious styling gels
but they're all parts of my tunnel through
time, just as much as the heroic version of
myself i could never quite catch up with. he
sure runs fast, fast as winter which arrives
earlier every year. the lab results came back:
turns out my blood is 96% over my credit limit
and 4% other. should our eyes open and meet,
our hearts high-five and grow wings, could we
then, pretty-please, hit the big reset button?
was the plan to salute the bedazzled twilight?
to be truly naked, and honest as a garden?
to stuff the self with pity until it explodes like a
volcano? a bomb's life is all about the waiting
and then kaboom! time bends; you can't say
goodbye fast enough. but what if everything
comes back, redeemed? snuff film reborn as
feathers, as hollow bird bones; wrong number
smelted down, recast as the song of the lark
announcing a face i'd thought i'd lost forever.
i run to the beach, wait for a wave i recognize.

First Date Frozen in Time's Infernal Football

we were fresh meat in the big city, we bought
tickets to an all-night filmfest, fell asleep just
after the zombie wrestled the shark. when we
awoke the master of ceremonies was foaming
at the mouth about 666 and black helicopters.
cousins i knew only vaguely were reproducing
at warp speed, a million bombs meant a million
votes and between us was a ghost with an itch
he just couldn't scratch. a derelict snored by our
feet, the cloud of blue smoke spilling out of the
balcony made me think of cotton candy and if
the ghost had told me that someday i'd look
back on that night with tears burning my eyes
i wouldn't have understood. makes me wonder
what magical bit of today i let slip right through
my fingers. now isn't much but it's all i ever
learned to trust, darrells of the past or future
have always been shifty as double agents. me
is what i call myself but honestly i feel like i'm
just an atom in a chain. time's raincoat is full of
secret pockets stuffed with oblivion's i.o.u.'s.
stereophonic voids haunt the present like
bottomless ditches haunt my life's highway.

Invisibility Diary

never would have guessed that the robot
monster was just a fuzzy gremlin with a
massive exoskeleton, or that i could sail
so far on one flimsy hummingbird's wing.
with a hatful of rain and a pocket full of
jokes, for decades i dodged bill collectors
until the landlord's guild put a sad emoji
on my file, called me the invisible man.
under the bridge there's a casket full of
geraniums, mountains of mismatched
shoes. when the economist called me a
lonely equation in a broken-hearted void
it hurt like a canker sore but i cheered
myself right back up by charting new
constellations for our brave new century:
orion the deadbeat dad, pegasus the
missing amazon package, cygnus the
downsized tech support associate.
some don't vibe my voodoo; some do.
all i ever wanted was forever, to have
my name carved in smoke, the smoke
on the finger-painted postcard of the
daily drone strike. 2025's a thunderbolt
reflected in an upside down teardrop.

Window Seat on the So Sorry Safari

the pantomime dance of my scars, my lapses
in judgment, the end times time table mapped
on the tablecloth, add up to blue checkmarks
in the win column. this is what i tell myself.
there's an alien logic key i use on special
occasions when i want to make the landlord
disappear, or chop up my anxiety into
bite-size pieces. surely mastercard will
wipe my slate clean once i sail out past the
van allen radiation belts. check the helmet,
the valves, the first aid kit, because you
can't go home again, and my old babysitter
lies for the ministry of truth now. down for
her is up. she let me watch tv past my
bedtime. mr. spock lay down his life for
his friends and she never shed a tear; i
never trusted her after that. if only my
words were magic, and love as easy as
rain. dead fractions caught in a butterfly
net—how i'd love to rehabilitate them with
duct tape and talk therapy. soul-winning
pamphlets and red-hot deals pile up
behind the door. i talk tough but even my
bazookas are made out of cotton candy.

Metal Angel Moonsault

after amalgamation, the benefits package was bare
bones. the dentist used a sharp stick and
a soldering iron. the doctor paused the exam to
ask the ghost of merlin for advice. there were
bloody stars and chicken bones on the carpet.
the fork in the road bloomed with false positives.
after y2k, dazzled by dreary axiom, science fiction
lost the plot. we packed the poor into a bullet train
screaming through the rust belt, their itinerary an
infernal mobius strip, sold ad space on satan's
clown car. i dreamed of a fresh start, a 10-ton
drum of liquid paper, wondered if capital one
would cancel my debt if i made it out past the
van allen radiation belts. better double-check
the valves, the o-rings, the first aid kit. tonight
a madman works on a pipe bomb time machine.
a lovely gesture but a long shot, like stealing a
truck and driving to lackawanna just to admire
the basilica, her huge bronze doors, the golden
bell they call the tintinnabulum. i returned it the
next day anyhow. there's a million ram-1500's
in the world but only one life and the rewind
button's just a prop. if i'd known i'd live this long
i would have held onto the instruction manual.

Just Like a Glacier and Yet Not Really

in restaurants she never entered i saw her ghost.
rented random basements, covered the floor with
mousetraps, hoping to catch her. ran faster, ran
slower, didn't matter. in a motel by the allegheny
i waited for the phone to ring, met kindred spirits,
kabuki phantoms yelling at traffic, but they never
had a clue. then one day psychosis like a cloud
just lazily sailed away, and i couldn't picture her.
the secret is: lean in to the ricochet, don't try to
fight it, and under every street's another street.
just because something doesn't exist doesn't
mean it didn't spike my drink at the new year's
eve party. i woke up in the wrong bathtub, with
fingernails that were six inches long. i'm always
changing, just like a river, still came in last in the
river look-alive contest. emily dickinson could
stare at a goldenrod head until all its essential
quantum fields were laid bare. harder trick to
pull off today: just ask cnn and fractional reserve
banking. a wise man's kindness is his monument:
he knows today's canoe is tomorrow's coffin.
the buried treasure we paved over. suspicious
fingerprints on every raindrop. a heart resting
on stilts that hardly ever touch the ground.

Dark Star Sunflower

pirouetting rates of decay,
geiger counter love letter,
dirty tricks the x-ray missed.
dog-faced drone, blotting out
the stars, the golden arches.
never warned me about the
bear traps, you wanted me to
read between the lines, and
why did the chicken cross the
road when he knew there was
nothing out there, everything
he'd ever wanted was behind
him, back inside the egg. not
easy to dream inside the womb
but i did it, still have the trophy.
easier than cartwheeling while
on fire, or tying a proper tie.
math, now that was tough.
and the star charts we had to
untangle, to bridge the gap
between what i meant and
what i said. even fiat currency
was in on it. the world wobbles
like the orbits of tipsy comets.

Virtual Tour Guide

here is where aphids breed in the night;
over there is where martin got busted
for driving with expired plates. when
lys was here, the mulberry cafe was
the place to be; hyperinflation turned
it into just another bad joke. luxury is
for the cloud-dwellers, not ward 3's
stick-man placeholders. cost benefit
analysis and nefarious sine waves
relocated us to somewhere between
abstraction and invisibility. here is a
screaming starling reminding me of
macbeth, here's a rip in the canopy
of sky. roar of the factory's mighty
stamping press, roar of the eyelid
slamming shut. some folks build body
doubles out of doll parts, hoping to
dodge the darts of a dark fate. and
don't try to help: my heart needs
these thorns just like a circle needs
the idea of a perfect circle, a distant
star to shoot for. some folks never
find their song. here is where i am:
hub of a great wheel forever turning.

Trumpet Without a Kickstand

an excruciating chasm swallows up the
punchline—is anyone out there at all? it's
ridiculous, this inhale-exhale flamenco
we're thrown into without ever signing a
single consent form! we're blinded by the
spotlight's glare, thrust onto the stage
with no time to learn our lines. should i
tell a joke, or turn a scarf into doves?
the audience hums, grows impatient,
so i break character, peel off the mask,
throw a noose around the sky, pretend
my camry's transmission will magically
heal itself. penny for your thoughts,
battle royal of ideal forms. trumpet
without a kickstand, windshield full
of spies. the sun like a burnt button,
my work history like a black hole's
autograph. goblins at the market
make us beg, turn us into snitches,
but even goblins can't stop a thistle
from growing out of the rubble.
at stage left, the future holds her
breath. for my last trick i knit the
thistle into a happy ending: ta da!

The author wishes to thank the editors of

The Eunoia Review
and
White Wall Review

where some of these poems first appeared.

For more information about Darrell Epp,
or to contact him for speaking engagements,
please visit him on X @DarrellEpp.

Many voices. One message.

www.quoir.com

www.ingramcontent.com/pod-product-compliance
Lightning Source LLC
Chambersburg PA
CBHW020754130626
46554CB00006B/2182